ISAAC ASIMOV'S NEW LIBRARY OF THE UNIVERSE

SPACE EXPLORERS

BY ISAAC ASIMOV
WITH REVISIONS AND UPDATING BY FRANCIS REDDY

Gareth Stevens Publishing
MILWAUKEE

For a free color catalog describing Gareth Stevens' list of high-quality books, call 1-800-542-2595 (USA) or 1-800-461-9120 (Canada). Gareth Stevens' Fax: (414) 225-0377.

Library of Congress Cataloging-in-Publication Data

Asimov, Isaac.
  Space explorers / by Isaac Asimov; with revisions and
updating by Francis Reddy.
     p. cm. — (Isaac Asimov's New library of the universe)
   Rev. ed. of: Piloted space flights. 1990.
   Includes index.
   ISBN 0-8368-1226-3
   1. Manned space flight—Juvenile literature. [1. Manned space
flight.] I. Reddy, Francis, 1959-. II. Asimov, Isaac. Piloted
space flights. III. Title. IV. Series: Asimov, Isaac. New library
of the universe.
TL793.A834 1995
629.45'009—dc20   95-7232

This edition first published in 1995 by
Gareth Stevens Publishing
1555 North RiverCenter Drive, Suite 201
Milwaukee, Wisconsin 53212, USA

Revised and updated edition © 1995 by Gareth Stevens, Inc.
Original edition published in 1990 by Gareth Stevens, Inc.
under the title *Piloted Space Flights.* Text © 1995 by Nightfall, Inc.
End matter and revisions © 1995 by Gareth Stevens, Inc.

Series editor: Barbara J. Behm
Design adaptation: Helene Feider
Production director: Teresa Mahsem
Editorial assistant: Diane Laska
Picture research: Matthew Groshek and Diane Laska

Printed in the United States of America

1 2 3 4 5 6 7 8 9 99 98 97 96 95

To bring this classic of young people's information up to date, the editors at Gareth Stevens Publishing have selected two noted science authors, Greg Walz-Chojnacki and Francis Reddy. Walz-Chojnacki and Reddy coauthored the recent book *Celestial Delights: The Best Astronomical Events Through 2001.*

Walz-Chojnacki is also the author of the book *Comet: The Story Behind Halley's Comet* and various articles about the space program. He was an editor of *Odyssey,* an astronomy and space technology magazine for young people, for eleven years.

Reddy is the author of nine books, including *Halley's Comet, Children's Atlas of the Universe, Children's Atlas of Earth Through Time,* and *Children's Atlas of Native Americans,* plus numerous articles. He was an editor of *Astronomy* magazine for several years.

CONTENTS

We live in an enormously large place – the Universe. It's just in the last fifty-five years or so that we've found out how large it probably is. It's only natural that we would want to understand the place in which we live, so scientists have developed instruments – such as radio telescopes, satellites, probes, and many more – that have told us far more about the Universe than could possibly be imagined.

We have seen planets up close. We have learned about quasars and pulsars, black holes, and supernovas. We have gathered amazing data about how the Universe may have come into being and how it may end. Nothing could be more astonishing.

The most amazing fact of all is that humans themselves have ventured into space. Not only have humans circled Earth in orbit many times and returned safely, they have even walked on another world! And today, humans actually live and work in space for long periods of time on space stations. What does the future of space exploration hold?

Isaac Asimov

Space Pioneers

The Chinese were using rockets over seven hundred years ago. But only within the the last few decades have scientists discovered how to launch rockets out of Earth's atmosphere and into space.

During World War II, the German scientist Wernher von Braun developed rockets that could travel hundreds of miles. After the war, rockets were made that could be launched higher and higher. In 1957, the former Soviet Union used a rocket to put a satellite into orbit.

If a satellite is large enough, it can carry humans. On April 12, 1961, a rocket ship from the Soviet Union carried Yuri Gagarin once around the world and back. He was the first person in space.

The first United States citizen in space was Alan B. Shepard. He was boosted 116 miles (187 kilometers) into space on May 5, 1961. On August 6, 1961, Gherman Titov of the Soviet Union completed seventeen orbits of Earth. U.S. space pioneer John H. Glenn circled Earth three times on February 20, 1962.

In Russia, space travelers are called cosmonauts. In the United States, they are called astronauts.

Left: A helicopter lifts U.S. astronaut Alan B. Shepard out of the Atlantic Ocean after his successful space flight in 1961.

Inset, left: The first human in space was cosmonaut Yuri Gagarin.

Inset, right: A chimpanzee named Ham was launched into space before any human.

Space Walking

Scientists have always hoped that astronauts would be able to work in space outside their ships, repairing satellites or building structures.

The first step toward this goal was a space walk on March 10, 1965, when cosmonaut Alexei Leonov set foot outside his spaceship. He was held to the ship by a rope called a tether. He wore a space suit that supplied heat, oxygen, and protection from harm. Leonov looked at the stars and at the Earth beneath him for ten minutes. On June 3, 1965, U.S. astronaut Edward H. White walked in space. He was also tethered and stayed outside his ship for twenty-one minutes.

Below: In 1984, U.S. astronauts Bruce McCandless and Robert Stewart briefly flew freely, without tethers, as they made successful tests of a new "jet-pack" that propelled them.

Right: U.S. astronaut Edward H. White takes a walk outside his capsule in 1965.

Inset: In 1984, the first woman to walk in space was cosmonaut Svetlana Savitskaya.

Stepping Toward the Moon

U.S. President John F. Kennedy wanted to see Americans on the Moon before the end of the 1960s. But it had to be done one step at a time.

In the early stages leading up to a Moon landing, the United States tested two-person ships in the *Gemini* program and three-person ships in the *Apollo* program. Rendezvous and docking procedures were developed, so two ships could approach each other and lock together. The first docking took place in March 1966 between *Gemini 8* and an unpiloted craft. Then, the United States began sending rocket ships toward the Moon. One ship was even sent around the Moon, skimming just above the lunar surface.

The Soviet Union wanted to be the first to put cosmonauts on the Moon, too. In 1959, they placed an unpiloted craft on the Moon's surface. But in 1969, the United States was ready for the big step.

Below, left: In the 1960s, the Unmanned Lunar Orbiter (U.S.) scanned the Moon for possible landing sites.

Below, right: This stamp from Poland shows a Soviet probe landing on the Moon in 1966.

Opposite: In 1969, *Apollo 12* astronauts landed about 600 feet (182 m) from the U.S. probe *Surveyor 3*, which had set down on the Moon two years earlier.

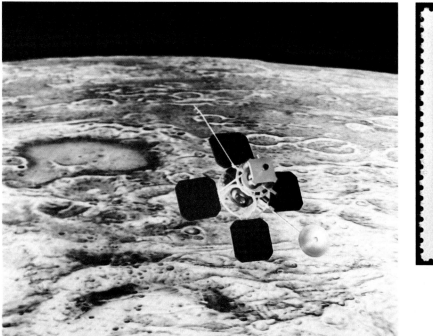

9

The Last Giant Leap

Finally, the U.S. spaceship *Apollo 11* was ready to land on the Moon. On board were three astronauts – Neil Armstrong, Edwin E. "Buzz" Aldrin, and Michael Collins. *Apollo 11* was launched on July 16, 1969.

Four days later, it entered into orbit around the Moon. As the lunar lander *Eagle* descended to the Moon's surface with Armstrong and Aldrin aboard, Collins remained in orbit aboard the command ship. On July 20, 1969, at 4:18 p.m. (Eastern Time), *Eagle* touched down on lunar soil. At 10:56 p.m., Neil Armstrong became the first human in history to set foot on the Moon. As he stepped down, millions of people listening to radio and television heard him say, "That's one small step for man, one giant leap for mankind."

Opposite: Buzz Aldrin adjusts experiments during *Apollo 11*'s visit to the lunar surface.

Below: President Nixon congratulates the crew of *Apollo 11*. The astronauts were isolated for a time after their return to protect against any alien germs.

? *Life out there? Let's take a look.*

Scientific instruments reveal there is no life on the Moon or Mars. Jupiter has a satellite, Europa, covered with ice. Might there be water under this glacier – and life within it? Saturn has a satellite, Titan, that has a thick atmosphere. Might there be some form of life on Titan's surface? Scientists will take a closer look some day.

Spaceship Recycling

In the early days of space flight, a rocket ship could be used only once. Advancements in technology, however, have made possible spaceships that can be launched, returned to Earth, and launched again and again. This type of ship is called a space shuttle.

The first U.S. space shuttle, *Columbia*, was launched on April 12, 1981 – twenty years to the day after Yuri Gagarin made his first flight.

On November 15, 1988, the Soviet Union launched its first shuttle. Called *Buran* (a Russian word for "blizzard"), the unpiloted shuttle was operated by remote control.

Opposite: The U.S. space shuttle *Discovery* lifts off from Cape Canaveral. *Inset:* Tests with early designs like this HL-10 Lifting Body helped shape the U.S. space shuttle.

Below: An artist's depiction of *Buran* as it leaves the launch pad. *Inset:* The European Space Agency is considering making a mini-shuttle named *Hermes*.

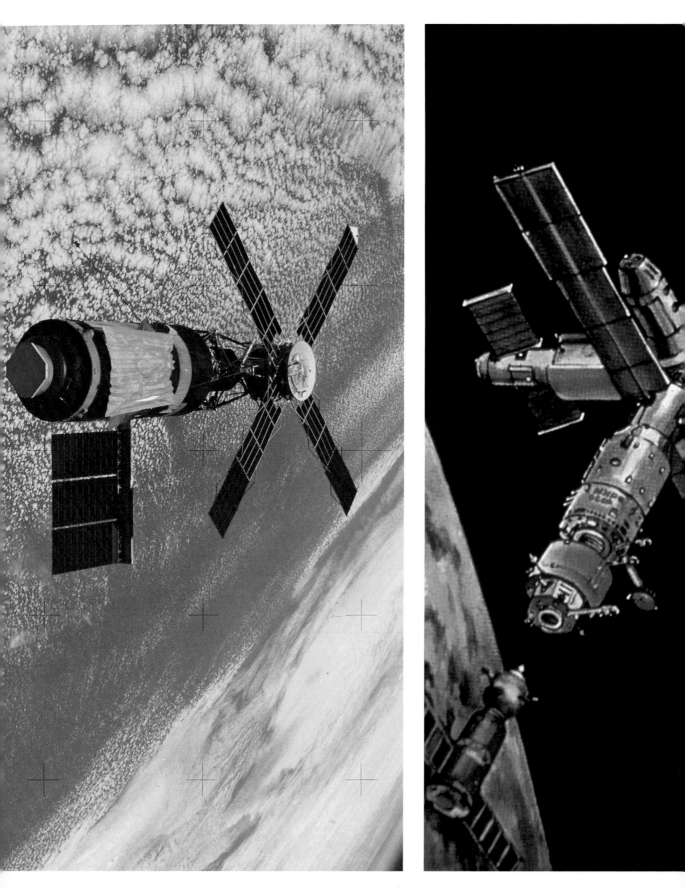

Space Station Advances

Russia has a space station, called *Mir* ("peace"), in orbit at this very moment. The first portion of *Mir* was launched in 1986. Modules were gradually added to it. A crew of cosmonauts stays there for up to a year at a time. Then a new crew replaces the previous crew. Unpiloted resupply ships bring oxygen, food, and equipment to *Mir*.

The first true space station, *Salyut 1*, was launched by the Soviet Union in 1971. Six others followed. The last *Salyut* fell back to Earth in 1991.

The only space station launched by the United States so far is *Skylab*. It was launched on May 14, 1973 and housed three crews from 1973-1974.

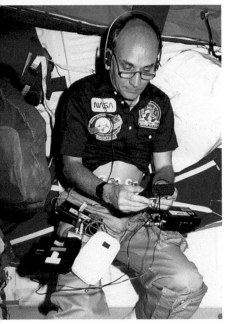

? *Weightlessness – not all it's cracked up to be?*

Fighting gravity keeps muscles strong and bones hard. In space, the body does not fight gravity. When cosmonauts have returned from months in space, they have had trouble standing up. When astronauts have been in space for several days, their bones have gotten thinner and their muscles flabbier. What will happen to people who are in space for years? In the future, spaceships may have to spin to produce false gravity.

Center: An illustration of the Russian space station *Mir*.

Left: U.S. Senator Jake Garn tests his body's responses to weightlessness.

Opposite: The U.S. *Skylab* space station.

15

Crews from All Walks of Life

The first U.S. astronauts were part of the military. They attended military test-pilot school and studied engineering or science. They had to understand complicated machinery. Because the first spaceships were quite small, they also had to be of medium height.

Later on, civilian test pilots were also chosen to be astronauts. In time, civilians without piloting experience could be astronauts, too. Eventually, even body size was not a factor. And finally, crews included civilians from the ranks of scientists, politicians, and teachers.

The selection of cosmonauts followed a similar pattern, although Russia led the way in putting women in space. The first female to orbit Earth was cosmonaut Valentina Tereshkova in 1963. The first female astronaut was Sally Ride, twenty years later.

Above: The first woman in space was cosmonaut Valentina Tereshkova in 1963.

Opposite, top: The crew of the U.S. space shuttle *Challenger* included teacher Christa McAuliffe. All seven astronauts lost their lives when their craft exploded in 1986. Pictured are *(front, left to right):* Michael J. Smith, Francis R. (Dick) Scobee, and Ronald E. McNair; *(back, left to right):* Ellison S. Onizuka, McAuliffe, Gregory Jarvis, and Judith A. Resnik.

Opposite, bottom: Cosmonauts and astronauts were on the same space mission in 1975. The mission was the *Apollo-Soyuz* Test Project. *Inset:* An *Apollo-Soyuz* patch.

❢ *International missions: Faster, friendlier, wiser*

Both the United States and Russia have had experience with piloted space flight, so both nations could contribute knowledge to a joint mission. In 1975, the two countries participated in a small, combined space mission called the Apollo-Soyuz Test Project. Now both nations plus Europe and Japan are involved in an international space station project.

16

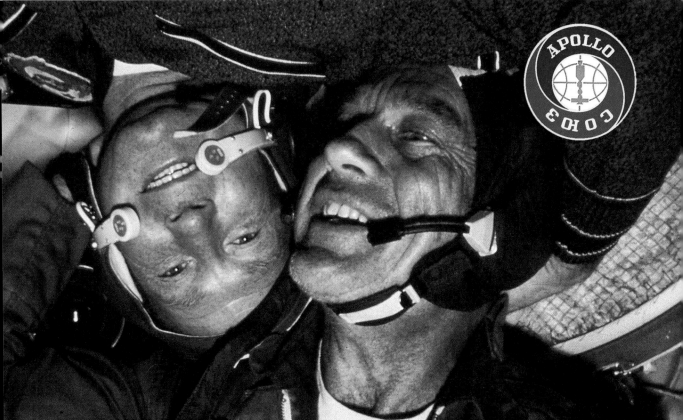

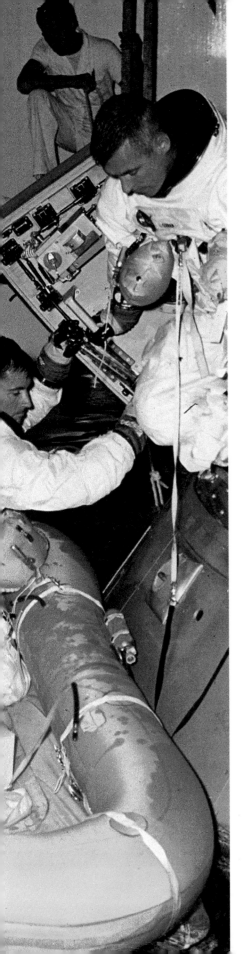

Going Through the Motions

Astronauts and cosmonauts must understand how the controls of a spaceship work as well as the science and engineering behind them. They must also be tested physically and psychologically for the special conditions of space flight.

Crew members experience high gravity when they take off and zero gravity in space. To help prepare them for high gravity, their training includes whirling speedily around and around. For low gravity, they train under water or they dive in airplanes. Astronauts/cosmonauts go through all the motions of space flight in make-believe spaceships on Earth.

Opposite: Astronaut candidates experience weightlessness in an airplane. The plane dives steeply toward the ground. This creates weightlessness in a brief "free fall."

Center: Apollo astronauts practice an ocean recovery procedure.

Below: Astronauts rehearse an EVA, or extravehicular activity, under water.

Surviving Long Journeys in Space

How well do humans manage in space? Shuttle flights and trips to the Moon usually take only a week or so, and people have managed that quite well. But to go beyond the Moon means that people will have to stay in spaceships longer.

How would humans fare on a one- or two-year trip to Mars and back? It is not known for certain, although Russia has successfully kept people in space for up to a year at a time.

And what about the spaceships themselves? After all, a ship must be able to support human beings for a long time. Oxygen, food, and water have to be supplied. Carbon dioxide has to be removed from the ship's "atmosphere." Wastes have to be recycled.

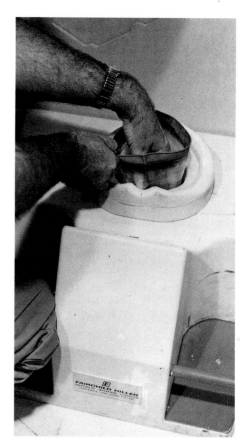

Top: A crew member replaces a space toilet bag in a training unit.

Bottom: This painting shows one of the main obstacles in a piloted mission to Mars — bringing along enough food, water, and oxygen for the two-year journey.

Opposite: This astronaut is about to eat a forkload of food that is floating before him. *Inset:* A *Skylab* food tray.

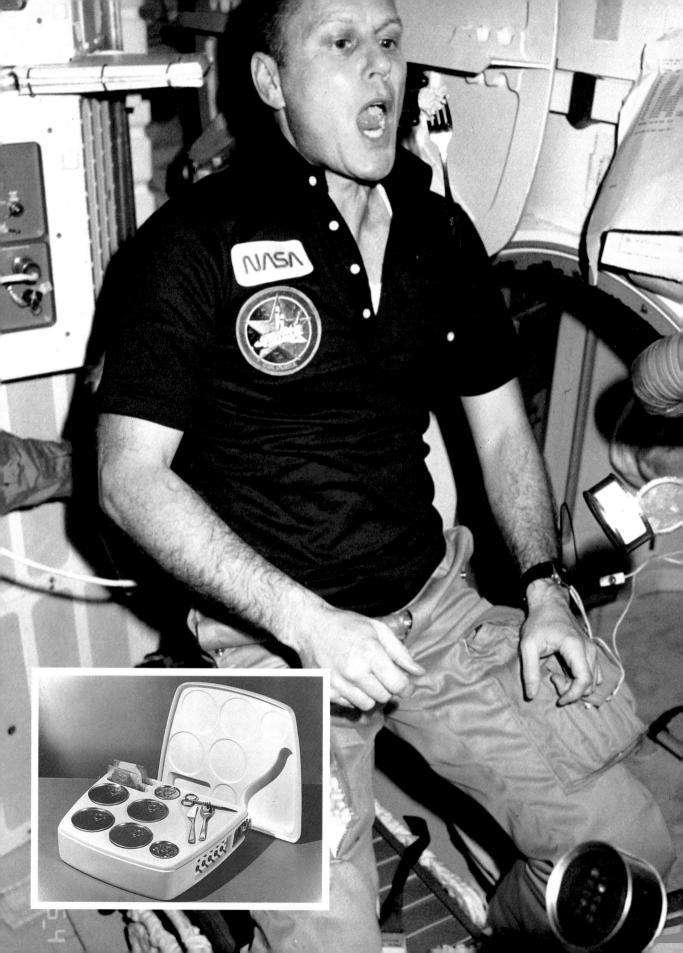

Mars – the Next Frontier?

The planets are a great deal farther away from Earth than the Moon. Venus is about 200 times as far away as the Moon. Mercury is farther still. Mars is 140 times as far away. Venus and Mercury are far too hot for human beings to land upon. Mars, however, is a different story.

Visiting Mars is quite possible. It will be a long, expensive, and dangerous trip, but both the United States and Russia are considering it.

Below, left: Under weightlessness, muscles weaken, the heart changes size, and the balance system of the inner ear may be affected. Even the human skeleton begins to break down.

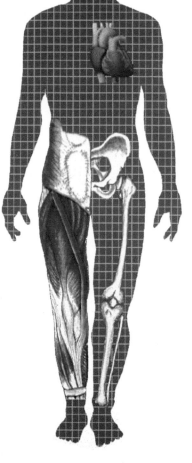

? ! *Space settlements – mobile homes to Mars?*

In the future, material from the Moon may be used to build huge settlements in orbit where thousands of people might live. Activities in these settlements will be similar to those on spaceships. The "space people" will need to be accustomed to space and space flight. They will need to adapt to low gravity and life-support systems.

Below: An artist's concept of a mining operation with drilling into the surface of Mars.
Inset: U. S. astronauts are greeted by a parade after their return to Earth.

Single Stage to Orbit

Even with reusable space shuttles, it is still very expensive to place astronauts and all they need to survive into orbit. Many scientists feel this can be accomplished much more efficiently with powerful launch vehicles designed as a single piece. Such rockets would blast people and supplies into orbit without having to throw away parts on the way, as all space vehicles – even the space shuttles – do today. This capability is called Single Stage to Orbit, or SSTO.

One concept, called the X-30, called for a vehicle that would take off like a plane from an airport runway, blast into orbit, and then return to a runway for landing. In 1993, the McDonnell Douglas Space Systems Company demonstrated a small prototype vehicle, called DC-X. It took off, hovered, moved horizontally, and then landed vertically on its legs! Developments like this will help bring down the cost of launches.

Opposite: The DC-X test vehicle is rolled out by McDonnell Douglas in 1993.

Below: The X-30, also known as the National Aerospace Plane, would take off and land at airports – but reach into orbit!

! *On to the stars*

Even the nearest star is about seven thousand times as far away as Pluto, the farthest known planet in our Solar System. Maybe the best way to visit the stars some day is for large settlements simply to drift through space with their generations of humans on board. These people probably wouldn't feel lost or lonely because they would be taking their home with them.
And what a view they'd be getting of the Universe!

The International Space Station

Long before astronauts are sent to other planets, scientists need to better understand how humans will adjust to conditions if they live and work in space over long periods. In the 1980s, the United States planned to construct a large space station, but it was considered too expensive. A newer design is a joint project between the U.S., Russia, and many other countries.

If all goes well, the first portions of the station will be launched into orbit in 1997. The station will be built in space over the following five years. After twenty U.S. space shuttle launches, over fifty Russian launches, and one European Space Agency launch, the new International Space Station will be complete.

*Robot explorers –
to boldly go . . .*

It is not possible for humans to travel everywhere. Temperatures on Venus are hot enough to melt tin and lead, and its atmosphere is poisonous. The giant planets have thick atmospheres that humans may not be able to enter. There may be a great deal of knowledge to be gained by using robots to go places where humans cannot.

Below, left: In this television image, U.S. astronaut Dr. Norman Thagard *(lower, right)* joined Russian cosmonauts on a mission to the Russian space station *Mir* in 1995. This was the first important step for international space station cooperation.

Below, right: This artwork shows the U.S. space shuttle *Atlantis* docked to the Russian *Mir* space station.

Opposite: The future International Space Station. Crews will be staying on board even before its completion.

Fact File: Space Camps

It's one thing to read about or watch movies about space exploration. But plunging into the sights, sounds, and other sensations of space travel is quite another story. The simple fact is that not everyone can take part in space flight – at least not yet.

However, many museums and space centers can give you a chance to experience some of the joys of space travel through camps, training simulators, and special shows.

On the next page is a list of some of these establishments. Their programs appeal to both children and adults. One thing to keep in mind is that the programs can be expensive.

Above and below: If you've ever dreamed of being an astronaut, space camps and future astronaut training programs will give you a chance to experience conditions beyond our Earth's atmosphere.

Future Astronaut Training Program

Hutchinson, Kansas

Five-day program:
- Space survival training
- Flight and Manned Maneuvering Unit (MMU) simulator workouts
- A simulated shuttle launch

Call **1-316-662-2305**, or write:
Future Astronaut Training Program
Kansas Cosmosphere and
  Space Center
1100 North Plum Street
Hutchinson, KS 67501

Space Camps

Huntsville, Alabama
Titusville, Florida
Yawata, Japan

Programs of varying lengths for children and adults:
- "Space walk" in a Manned Maneuvering Unit (MMU) simulator
- Multi-axis simulator that rotates in every direction to create the disorienting, sometimes wild, feeling of navigating a craft
- Simulated shuttle launch, with group members taking turns acting as shuttle crew and mission control members
- "Space Habitat" housing that looks like a NASA space station
- In U.S.: tours of nearby Alabama Space and Rocket Center and NASA Marshall Space Flight Center (Alabama) and NASA Kennedy Space Center (Florida)
- In Japan: in addition to simulators and dorms similar to those in the U.S., there are rides, a museum, and a space theater

Call **1-800-63SPACE**, or write:
Alabama Space and Rocket Center
Space Camp Applications
P. O. Box 070015
Huntsville, AL 35807-7015

Michigan Space Center

Jackson, Michigan

Week-long day camp:
- Building model rockets from scratch
- Visiting a planetarium
- Airport field trip
- Stargazing on a Friday night sleep-over (optional for eighth graders)

Call **1-517-787-4425**, or write:
Michigan Space Center
2111 Emmons Road
Jackson, MI 49201

Challenger Centers for Space Science Education

Houston, Texas
Washington, D.C.
(Many more sites are
under consideration)

- Simulated work places and space habitats, such as a mission control center and space station
- A variety of "missions" lasting from several hours to several days. Among existing or planned "missions"– a trip to the Moon and a space station rendezvous with Halley's Comet
- Evening and weekend space science classes for children and adults

Call **1-202-484-0652**, or write:
Challenger Center for
  Space Science Education
RD and T Center
8th and H Street SW
Washington, D.C. 20024

Shuttle Camp

Alamogordo, New Mexico

Day camp or overnight programs:
- Building and launching model rockets
- Eating space food
- Handling actual space hardware, such as shuttle tiles and space helmets
- Underwater zero-gravity simulations
- Field trips to nearby White Sands Missile Range and Holloman Air Force Base

Call **1-800-545-4021**, or write:
Shuttle Camp / Space Center
P. O. Box 533
Alamogordo, NM 88311

More Books about Exploring Space

Global Space Programs. Asimov (Gareth Stevens)
How Do You Go to the Bathroom in Space? Pogue (TOR Books)
Out of the Cradle: Exploring the Frontiers Beyond Earth. Hartmann (Workman)
Space Colonies. Asimov (Gareth Stevens)
Sputnik to Space Shuttle: The Complete Story of Space Flight. Nicolson (Dodd, Mead)

Videos

Astronomy 101: A Beginner's Guide to the Night Sky. (Mazon)
Astronomy Today. (Gareth Stevens)
There Goes a Spaceship. (KidVision)

Places to Visit

You can explore space without leaving Earth. Here are some museums and centers where you
can find a variety of space exhibits.

National Air and Space Museum
Smithsonian Institution
Seventh and Independence Avenue SW
Washington, D.C. 20560

San Diego Aero-Space Museum
2001 Pan American Plaza
Balboa Park
San Diego, CA 92101

Seneca College Planetarium
1750 Finch Avenue East
North York, Ontario M2J 2X5

Anglo-Australian Observatory
Private Bag
Coonarbariban 2357 Australia

Hayden Planetarium
Museum of Science
Science Park
Boston, MA 02114-1099

Henry Crown Science Center
Museum of Science and Industry
57th Street and Lake Shore Drive
Chicago, IL 60637

Places to Write

Here are some places you can write for more information about space exploration. Be sure to
state what kind of information you would like. Include your full name and address so they can
write back to you.

National Space Society
922 Pennsylvania Avenue SE
Washington, D.C. 20003

The Planetary Society
65 North Catalina
Pasadena, CA 91106

Canadian Space Agency
Communications Department
6767 Route de L'Aeroport
Saint Hubert, Quebec J3Y 8Y9

Sydney Observatory
P. O. Box K346
Haymarket 2000 Australia

Glossary

alien: in this book, a being from a place other than Earth.

Apollo 11: the first piloted vehicle to land on the Moon. On July 20, 1969, Neil Armstrong became the first person to walk on the Moon.

Apollo-Soyuz: a mission where *Apollo* (U.S.) and *Soyuz* (Soviet Union) linked together in a joint orbital endeavor in 1975. Three U.S. astronauts met two Soviet cosmonauts in orbit, shook hands, and conducted experiments together.

astronaut: a person from the U.S. who travels beyond Earth's atmosphere.

atmosphere: the gases that surround a planet, star, or moon.

carbon dioxide: along with nitrogen, one of the main gases that made up Earth's atmosphere early in the history of our planet. It is a heavy, colorless gas. Carbon dioxide is what gives soda its fizz. When humans and animals breathe, they exhale carbon dioxide.

civilian: someone who lives in a country but is not on active duty in its military, police, or firefighting force.

comet: an object made of ice, rock, and gas. It has a vapor tail that may be seen when the comet's orbit brings it close to the Sun.

cosmonaut: a person from Russia (the former Soviet Union) who travels beyond Earth's atmosphere.

glacier: an enormous layer of ice formed from compacted snow, often itself carrying a layer of snow.

gravity: the force that causes objects like the Earth and Moon to be attracted to one another.

NASA: the space agency in the United States – the National Aeronautics and Space Administration.

orbit: the path that one celestial object follows as it circles, or revolves, around another.

politician: a person who runs for or holds a governmental office.

satellite: a smaller body orbiting a larger body. The Moon is Earth's natural satellite. *Sputnik 1* and *2* were Earth's first artificial satellites.

space shuttles: rocket ships that can be used over and over again, since they return to Earth after completing their missions.

space stations: artificial structures in space in which humans can live and work, often for long periods of time.

space walk: an extravehicular (outside of the vehicle) venture made by an astronaut in space.

World War II: the second war fought by most of the principal nations of the world during the first half of the twentieth century.

zero gravity: weightlessness.

Index

Born in 1920, Isaac Asimov came to the United States as a young boy from his native Russia. As a young man, he was a student of biochemistry. In time, he became one of the most productive writers the world has ever known. His books cover a spectrum of topics, including science, history, language theory, fantasy, and science fiction. His brilliant imagination gained him the respect and admiration of adults and children alike. Sadly, Isaac Asimov died shortly after the publication of the first edition of *Isaac Asimov's Library of the Universe.*

The publishers wish to thank the following for permission to reproduce copyright material: front cover, NASA; 4 (left), James Oberg Archive; 4 (right), 4-5, 6, 6-7, NASA; 7, James Oberg Archive; 8, 9 (left), NASA; 9 (right), Collection of Ken Novak; 10, 11, NASA; 12 (large), Courtesy of Rockwell International; 12 (inset), NASA; 13 (large), © Paul Dimare; 13 (inset), Courtesy of European Space Agency (ESA); 14, NASA; 14-15, James Oberg Archive; 15, NASA; 16, James Oberg Archive; 17 (all), 18, 18-19, NASA; 19, Courtesy of McDonnell Douglas Astronautics Company; 20 (upper), NASA; 20 (lower), © Rick Karpinski/DeWalt and Associates 1989; 21 (both), NASA; 22, © Garret Moore 1989; 22-23, Pat Rawlings/Courtesy of NASA; 23, NASA; 24, Courtesy of McDonnell Douglas Corporation; 25, 26 (both), 27, NASA; 28 (all), Society of Space Development.

DATE DUE